101 Things
To Do With A
Salad

101 Things To Do With A Salad

BY
MELISSA BARLOW AND
STEPHANIE ASHCRAFT

Gibbs Smith, Publisher
Salt Lake City

First Edition
10 09 08 07 06   20 19 18 17 16 15 14 13 12 11 10 9 8 7 6 5 4 3 2 1

Published by
Gibbs Smith, Publisher
P.O. Box 667
Layton, Utah 84041

Orders: 1.800.748.5439
www.gibbs-smith.com

Designed by Kurt Wahlner
Printed and bound in Korea

Library of Congress Cataloging-in-Publication Data

Barlow, Melissa.
   101 things to do with a salad / Melissa Barlow and Stephanie Ashcraft.—
1st ed.
      p. cm.
   ISBN 1-4236-0013-4
   1. Salads. 1. Title: One hundred one things to do with a salad. II.
Ashcraft, Stephanie. III. Title.

TX740.B376 2006
641.8'3—dc22

2005025799

To my husband, Todd, for being so
supportive and always willing to
taste-test—I love you! And also to my
friends and family—thank you for
sharing your recipes with me.
—M. B.

This book is dedicated to lifelong friends.
To Erin Cramer and Kristen Cheek,
thank you for helping me survive Indiana
with such great memories and for
supporting me in my beliefs. To Paula
Taylor, the queen of salads, thank you
for always being my personal motivator
and cheering section. Thank you for the
many hours of service you have
given on my behalf.
—S. A.

CONTENTS

Helpful Hints 9

Leafy Salads

Summer Salad 12 • Spinach and Mushroom Salad 13 • Sweet Fiesta Salad 14 • Cranberry Spring Mix Salad 15 • Apple-Pear Salad 16 • Cherry-Swiss Salad 17 • Mandarin-Almond Salad 18 • Ranch-Sunflower Salad 19 • Bridal Shower Salad 20 • Raspberry-Chicken Salad 21 • Candy Bar Salad 22 • Strawberry-Spinach Salad with Lemon Dressing 23 • Lettuce Wedges 24 • Classic Italian Salad 25

Main Course Salads

Country Cobb Salad 28 • Chunky Chicken Pasta Salad 29 • Spicy Taco Salad 30 • Chinese Chicken Salad 31 • Crispy Chicken Salad 32 • Chicken Fajita Salad 33 • Chef Salad 34 • BBQ Chicken Salad 35 • Marinated Beef Salad 36 • Jo's Chicken Wonton Salad 37 • Enchilada Salad 38 • Avocado Chicken Caesar Salad 39 • Fruit 'n' Nut Chicken Salad 40 • Tortellini Salad 41 • Mango Chicken Salad 42

Pasta Salads

Jenny's Cashew Bow-Tie Pasta 44 • Pizza Pasta Salad 45 • Shrimp 'n' Seashell Salad 46 • Perfect Picnic Pasta Salad 47 • Chicken Caesar Pasta Salad 48 • Tuna Noodle Pasta Salad 49 • Classic Macaroni Salad 50 • Southwest Pasta Salad 51 • Bacon Ranch Pasta Salad 52 • Fruity Bow-Tie Pasta Salad 53 • Angie's Balsamic Chicken Pasta Salad 54 • Ranch Shell Pasta Salad 55 • Summer Feta Pasta Salad 56 • Red Potato–Pasta Salad 57 • Tangy Tricolor Pasta Salad 58 • Primavera Pasta Salad 59

BBQ and Picnic Salads

Mom's Potato Salad 62 • German Potato Salad 63 • Baked Potato Salad 64 • Chicken and Grape Salad 65 • Egg Salad with Bacon 66 • Hawaiian Coleslaw 67

• Oriental Cashew Coleslaw 68 • Mom's Tuna Salad 69 • Easy Crab Salad 70 • Turkey and Apple Salad 71

Veggie Salads

Tomato and Mozzarella Salad 74• Chilled Cucumber Salad 75 • Fruity Broccoli Salad 76 • Chunky Veggie Salad 77 • Four-Bean Salad 78 • Cauliflower-Shrimp Salad 79 • Crunchy Pea Salad 80 • Bacon Broccoli Salad 81 • Cauliflower–Green Pea Salad 82 • Mexicorn Bean Salad 83 • Ensalada Chilena 84 • Bell Pepper Salad 85 • Ranch Cauliflower and Broccoli Salad 86

Fruit Salads

Sweet-and-Sour Fruit Salad 88 • Melissa's Creamy Fruit Salad 89 • Cool Pear Salad 90 • Berries 'n' Crème Salad 91 • Puckered-Up Citrus Salad 92 • Melon Delight Salad 93 • Strawberry–Sour Cream Salad 94 • Cherry Waldorf Salad 95 • Dad's Favorite Fruit Salad 96 • Honey-Lime Fruit Salad 97 • Layered Fruit Salad 98 • Grape Nuts Salad 99 • Mango Fruit Salad 100 • Almond Cran-Apple Salad 101 • Strawberry-Banana Salad 102 • Fanciful Fruit Salad 103 • Poppy Seed–Cantaloupe Salad 104

Dessert Salads

Pistachio Salad 106 • Fluffy Lime Salad 107 • Dreamy Gelatin Salad 108 • Banana Cream Salad 109 • Jessica's Citrus Cream Salad 110 • Best Ever Frog-Eye Salad 111 • Rocky Road Salad 112 • Snickers Salad 113 • Refreshing Ice Cream Salad 114 • Cherry-Pineapple Salad 115 • Tropical Ambrosia Salad 116 • Peachy Gelatin Salad 117 • Grandma's Strawberry Pretzel Salad 118 • Grandma Dircks' Orange Cream Salad 119 • Tropical Cookie Salad 120 •Pineapple Pretzel Salad 121

Bonus Section: Dressings

Family Favorite Dressing 124 • Lime Vinaigrette Dressing 124 • Honey Mustard Dressing 124 • Creamy Italian Dressing 125 • Quick French Dressing 125 • Creamy Raspberry Dressing 125 • Creamy Parmesan Dressing 126 • Classic Vinaigrette Dressing 126 • Mom's Western Dressing 126

HELPFUL HINTS

1. Green-leaf salads should be assembled close to serving time. Dressings should be added right before serving to prevent salads from wilting.

2. To reduce calories, use low-fat or nonfat products.

3. Dip sliced, diced, or chopped pears, apples, and bananas in lemon juice to prevent them from turning brown.

4. Don't store tomatoes in the refrigerator. They last longer and taste fresher when stored on the kitchen counter out of direct sunlight. Do not wash tomatoes until ready to serve.

5. Bigger bowls work best for evenly tossing salads. To toss a salad, add ingredients, place a lid on the bowl, and give the bowl a few shakes.

6. To remove dirt and sand, soak leafy greens in ice-cold water right after they are brought home from the store. Lay greens over paper towels to dry. Place dry greens in an airtight bag lined with a paper towel and store in the vegetable compartment of a refrigerator until ready to serve. Use these cleaned greens within five days to assure freshness.

7. Salad spinners work well to clean lettuce. Simply tear your lettuce into bite-size pieces and drop into the spinner. Run cool water over the top of the torn lettuce, place the lid on the spinner, and spin at will. Your lettuce will come out clean and dry.

8. Thoroughly wash fruits and vegetables before peeling and cutting them. Fruits grown on a tree and berries should not be washed until you are ready to use them.

9. Cut cherry tomatoes and grapes in half before adding them to salads. Remember, bite-size pieces are easier for everyone to eat.

10. To keep cooked pastas from sticking together while cooling, sprinkle with a little olive oil and toss to coat.

11. Fresh heads of lettuce last longer than bagged, ready-to-serve lettuce.

12. Most green-leaf salads look nicer on individual serving plates instead of a large serving bowl.

13. When cooking meats to use in salads, don't be afraid to season them well—even if the recipe doesn't call for it. Adding a few different spices can give your meat and salad a more robust flavor.

LEAFY SALADS

SUMMER SALAD

Dressing:

1	**lemon,** juiced (3 to 4 tablespoons)
3	**cloves garlic,** crushed
1 teaspoon	**salt**
1/2 teaspoon	**pepper**
3/4 cup	**light olive oil**

Salad:

2	**small heads romaine lettuce,** torn into bite-size pieces
1/2 to 1 pound	**bacon,** cooked and crumbled
1 1/2 to 2 cups	**chopped tomatoes**
3/4 cup	**sunflower seeds**
1 cup	**grated Swiss cheese**
1/3 cup	**grated Parmesan cheese**
	croutons

In a bowl, combine dressing ingredients and set aside.

Combine all salad ingredients except croutons in a large bowl. When ready to serve, pour dressing over salad and toss. Sprinkle croutons over top. Makes 10–12 servings.

SPINACH AND MUSHROOM SALAD

Dressing:

1 1/2 teaspoons	**poppy seeds**
3/4 cup	**white distilled vinegar**
1 cup	**light olive oil**
3/4 cup	**sugar**
1 1/2 teaspoons	**salt**
3/4 teaspoon	**dry mustard**

Salad:

3/4 pound	**sliced mushrooms**
1	**red onion,** thinly sliced
1 bag (10 ounces)	**fresh spinach leaves**
1	**head iceberg lettuce,** chopped
1/2 to 1	**pound bacon,** cooked and crumbled
1 cup	**cottage cheese**
1 1/2 cups	**grated Swiss cheese**

Combine dressing ingredients in a bowl. Add mushrooms and onion and then cover. Refrigerate dressing 24 hours or at least overnight.

Mix all remaining salad ingredients in a bowl. When ready to serve, pour dressing over salad and toss. Makes 10–12 servings.

SWEET FIESTA SALAD

1 **large head romaine lettuce,** torn into
bite-size pieces
1 can (15 ounces) **red kidney beans,** rinsed and drained
1 cup **canned black beans,** rinsed and drained
1/2 **red onion,** thinly sliced
2 cups **grated cheddar cheese**
1 bottle (16 ounces) **Catalina dressing**
1 bag (10 ounces) **Fritos corn chips**

In a bowl, combine all ingredients except dressing and chips. When
ready to serve, pour dressing and chips over top. Add the dressing
gradually. You may not need to use it all. Toss until completely covered. Makes 10–12 servings.

VARIATION: Add 1 tomato, diced, and 3/4 cup sliced black olives.

14

CRANBERRY
SPRING MIX SALAD

1 bag (10 ounces) **Spring Mix salad**
1 bag (10 ounces) **Leafy Romaine salad**
1 bag (10 ounces) **Coleslaw salad**
1 bag (6 ounces) **dried cranberries**
1 to 1¹/₂ cups **candied or toffee nuts**
1 bottle (12 ounces) **poppy seed dressing**

Combine all ingredients except nuts and dressing in a large bowl.
When ready to serve, sprinkle nuts over salad and pour dressing over
top. Toss until completely covered. Makes 10–12 servings.

APPLE-PEAR SALAD

Dressing:

$^1/_2$ cup **lemon juice**

I tablespoon **Dijon mustard**

$^1/_2$ teaspoon **salt**

3 to 4 tablespoons **sugar**

$^2/_3$ cup **light olive oil**

I tablespoon **poppy seeds**

Salad:

2 **pears,** peeled and diced

2 **Granny Smith apples,** peeled and diced

I bag (10 ounces) **romaine lettuce**

I bag (10 ounces) **Spring Mix salad**

1 $^1/_2$ cups **grated Swiss cheese**

I cup **dried cranberries**

I cup **cashew halves**

Combine dressing ingredients in a bowl. Add pears and apples to keep from browning, then set aside.

In a large bowl, combine remaining salad ingredients. When ready to serve, pour dressing over top and toss until completely covered. Makes 10–12 servings.

CHERRY-SWISS SALAD

Dressing:

1 cup	**cider vinegar**
1/2 cup	**sugar**
1 teaspoon	**dry mustard**
2 teaspoons	**poppy seeds**

Salad:

2 to 3 tablespoons	**sugar**
1/2 cup	**sliced almonds**
2 bags (10 ounces each)	**romaine lettuce**
1 1/2 cups	**grated Swiss cheese**
1 cup	**dried cherries,** chopped

Combine dressing ingredients in a bowl and set aside.

In a small frying pan, melt sugar over low to medium heat. Add almonds and stir until sugar-coated. Cool and set aside. Mix all remaining salad ingredients in a bowl. When ready to serve, pour dressing over top and toss until completely covered. Sprinkle sugared almonds over top. Makes 10–12 servings.

MANDARIN-ALMOND SALAD

Dressing:

1/4 cup	**light olive oil**
3 to 4 tablespoons	**sugar**
2 tablespoons	**vinegar**
1 1/2 teaspoons	**dried parsley**
1/2 teaspoon	**salt**
	pepper, to taste
	Tabasco sauce, to taste

Salad:

3 tablespoons	**sugar**
1/2 cup	**sliced almonds**
1	**large head romaine lettuce**
1 can (6 ounces)	**mandarin oranges,** drained
1	**small red onion,** sliced
1 cup	**chow mein noodles**
1 cup	**chopped celery**

Combine all dressing ingredients in a bowl and set aside.

In a small frying pan, melt sugar over low to medium heat. Add almonds and stir until sugar-coated. Cool and set aside. Mix all remaining salad ingredients in a bowl. Pour dressing over top and toss. Sprinkle sugared almonds over top. Makes 10–12 servings.

RANCH-SUNFLOWER SALAD

1 **head romaine lettuce,** torn into bite-size pieces
1 1/2 cups **sugar snap peas,** halved
3/4 cup **grated carrots**
3/4 cup **sliced celery**
1 1/2 cups **grated sharp cheddar cheese**
3 **hard-boiled eggs,** sliced or chopped
3/4 cup **sunflower seeds**
1 bottle **ranch dressing**

In a large bowl, layer lettuce, peas, carrots, celery, cheese, and eggs. Sprinkle sunflower seeds over top. Toss just before serving, or leave layered. Serve with ranch dressing on the side. Makes 8–10 servings.

BRIDAL SHOWER SALAD

$1/2$ cup **mayonnaise**
$1/4$ cup **sugar**
$1/4$ cup **milk**
1 tablespoon **poppy seeds**
2 tablespoons **white or red wine vinegar**
1 **large head romaine lettuce,** torn into
    bite-size pieces
1 pint **strawberries,** sliced
$1/2$ **red onion,** thinly sliced
1 to $1 1/2$ cups **red grape halves**

In a bowl, combine mayonnaise, sugar, milk, poppy seeds, and vinegar. Mix well and chill.

In a large bowl, combine lettuce, strawberries, onion, and grapes. Pour dressing over top and toss just before serving. Makes 8–10 servings.

RASPBERRY-CHICKEN SALAD

2	**boneless, skinless chicken breasts,** cubed
	olive oil
I tablespoon	**honey**
I tablespoon	**minced garlic**
	salt and pepper, to taste
I cup	**plain yogurt**
I to 2 teaspoons	**red wine vinegar**
1/2 cup	**raspberries**
2 tablespoons	**sugar**
I	**head romaine lettuce,** torn into bite-size pieces
I bag (10 ounces)	**Spring Mix salad**
3/4 cup	**chopped celery**
1 1/2 cups	**fresh raspberries**
3/4 cup	**candied or toffee nuts**

In a frying pan, brown chicken in oil, honey, garlic, salt, and pepper. When done, set aside to cool.

In a blender, mix yogurt, vinegar, raspberries, and sugar together and then set dressing aside.

In a large bowl, combine lettuce, Spring Mix salad, celery, raspberries, and nuts. Sprinkle cooled chicken over top and serve dressing on the side. Makes 8–10 servings.

CANDY BAR SALAD

Salad:

2 pints	**fresh strawberries,** sliced
I bag (10 ounces)	**romaine lettuce**
I bag (10 ounces)	**fresh spinach or Spring Mix salad**
3	**Heath candy bars,** crushed

Dressing:

I cup	**mayonnaise**
$^1/_2$ cup	**milk**
$^1/_4$ cup	**white vinegar**
$^2/_3$ cup	**sugar**
2 tablespoons	**poppy seeds**

In a bowl, combine salad ingredients and toss.

In a separate bowl, combine dressing ingredients. Pour dressing over salad just before serving and toss to coat. Makes 8–10 servings.

STRAWBERRY-SPINACH SALAD WITH LEMON DRESSING

Salad:

1 cup **slivered almonds,** sugared
1 bag (10 ounces) **fresh spinach**
1 1/2 **apples,** peeled and cut into wedges
1 cup **dried cranberries**
2 cups **sliced strawberries**

Dressing:

2 tablespoons **lemon zest**
2 tablespoons **lemon juice**
1/4 cup **oil**
1/3 cup **sugar**
1 teaspoon **mustard seed** (optional)

Preheat oven to 350 degrees. To candy almonds, wet them and roll in sugar. Bake 10 minutes. Cool.

In a bowl, toss all salad ingredients together. In a separate bowl, combine dressing ingredients. Pour dressing over salad just before serving and toss. Makes 6–8 servings.

LETTUCE WEDGES

I small **head iceberg lettuce,** cut in 4–6 wedges
$3/4$ to I cup **blue cheese dressing**
$1/2$ cup **crumbled blue cheese**
salt and pepper, to taste
4 to 6 slices **bacon,** cooked

Place individual lettuce wedges on salad plates and evenly drizzle blue cheese dressing over top. Sprinkle with cheese, salt, and pepper. Crumble one piece of bacon over each salad wedge. Makes 4–6 servings.

VARIATION: Other dressing and cheese combinations are Caesar and grated Asiago cheese, ranch and grated cheddar cheese, and Italian and crumbled feta cheese.

CLASSIC ITALIAN SALAD

I bag (12 ounces) **Dole American blend salad**
 1/3 **red onion,** thinly sliced
 25 **pitted black olives**
 2 to 4 **small pepperoncini yellow peppers***
 6 to 8 **cherry tomatoes**
 1/2 cup **croutons**
 I bottle (8 ounces) **Italian salad dressing**
 Parmesan cheese, freshly grated

Place bag of salad in a serving bowl. Layer red onion, black olives, peppers, tomatoes, and croutons. Toss and serve with Italian salad dressing. Garnish with Parmesan cheese. Makes 3–4 servings.

*These peppers are usually found in a jar in the condiments aisle of the grocery store.

Main Course
Salads

COUNTRY COBB SALAD

1 bag (10 ounces)	**mixed salad greens**
3	**chicken breasts,** cooked and sliced
1	**large tomato,** cubed
1/2 cup	**sliced black olives**
1	**avocado,** peeled, seeded, and cubed
4	**hard-boiled eggs,** sliced
12 slices	**bacon,** cooked and crumbled
1 cup	**crumbled blue cheese**

In a large bowl, layer ingredients as listed above. Serve with a dressing of choice on the side. For individual salads, equally divide mixed greens onto plates, then layer with remaining ingredients. Makes 4–6 servings.

CHUNKY CHICKEN PASTA SALAD

2 cups **dry large-shell pasta,** cooked and cooled
3 **chicken breasts,** cooked and cubed
1 can (8 ounces) **pineapple tidbits,** drained
1 cup **unpeeled Gala apples,** chopped
1 cup **seedless red grapes,** halved
1 cup **diced celery**
2 tablespoons **finely chopped onion**
1 cup **cashews**
$^1/_2$ cup **coleslaw dressing**
$^1/_2$ cup **mayonnaise**
salt and pepper, to taste

Combine cooked pasta, chicken, fruit, celery, onion, and cashews in a bowl.

In a separate bowl, mix dressing and mayonnaise. Stir into salad mixture. Add more dressing, if desired. Season with salt and pepper. Makes 8–10 servings.

VARIATION: You may use 1 cup coleslaw dressing and eliminate the mayonnaise.

SPICY TACO SALAD

I pound **ground beef,** browned and drained
I envelope **taco seasoning**
1 1/2 cups **chunky salsa**
1/2 teaspoon **garlic powder**
salt and pepper, to taste
tortilla chips
2 cups **grated cheddar cheese**
1/2 to I **head iceberg lettuce,** shredded
2 **tomatoes,** diced
sour cream and guacamole (optional)

In a large frying pan, combine cooked beef, taco seasoning, salsa, garlic powder, salt, and pepper until completely heated through.

For individual servings, scoop meat mixture over a bed of tortilla chips on a plate. Layer remaining ingredients over top in order listed above. Makes 4 servings.

CHINESE CHICKEN SALAD

Dressing:

           1 cup **water**
           $^1/_3$ cup **rice vinegar**
           $^1/_3$ cup **olive oil**
           1 cup **sugar**
           1 packet **oriental ramen noodle seasoning**

Salad:

           1 **head cabbage,** thinly sliced or shredded
           2 stalks **celery,** sliced
           3 packages **oriental ramen noodles,** broken up
           2 cups **chicken,** cooked and cubed*
           $^1/_2$ cup **slivered almonds**
           $^1/_2$ cup **sunflower seeds**

Mix all dressing ingredients in a bowl and set aside. Combine salad ingredients in a bowl. Pour dressing over salad and toss until completely covered. Let stand in refrigerator 1–2 hours before serving. Makes 4–6 servings.

* Canned chicken may be used.

CRISPY CHICKEN SALAD

1 bag (28 ounces) **frozen crispy chicken strips**
1 bag (10 ounces) **romaine lettuce**
$^1/_2$ **red onion,** thinly sliced
6 to 8 **hard-boiled eggs,** sliced
12 slices **bacon,** cooked and crumbled
2 cups **grated sharp cheddar cheese**
ranch or honey mustard dressing

Bake chicken according to package directions. Equally divide lettuce onto plates. Layer onion, eggs, bacon, and cheese over top. Evenly divide cooked chicken strips and lay over top. Serve with ranch or honey mustard dressing, or both on the side. Makes 4–6 servings.

CHICKEN FAJITA SALAD

1 pound	**boneless, skinless chicken breasts,** cubed
1 envelope	**fajita seasoning**
1 bag (10 ounces)	**romaine lettuce**
1	**red bell pepper,** diced
1	**green bell pepper,** diced
1/2 to 1	**red onion,** thinly sliced
1 to 2	**limes,** quartered
1 cup	**grated cheddar or pepper jack cheese**
	tortilla chips, crushed
	ranch dressing
	salsa

Place chicken in a large zipper-lock bag. Marinate in fajita seasoning according to package directions.

In a frying pan, saute chicken until done. Equally divide lettuce on individual plates, and then evenly sprinkle bell peppers and onion over lettuce. Layer cooked chicken over top. Squeeze lime juice over each salad. Sprinkle cheese and tortilla chips over top. Serve with ranch dressing and salsa on the side. Makes 4–6 servings.

VARIATION: Layer 1 can (15 ounces) of rinsed and drained black beans over lettuce before chicken is added.

CHEF SALAD

2 bags (10 to 12 ounces each)	**mixed salad greens or romaine lettuce**
2 cups	**sliced deli turkey,** cut in $^1/_2$-inch strips
2 cups	**sliced deli ham,** cut in $^1/_2$-inch strips
1$^1/_2$ cups	**grated sharp cheddar cheese**
1$^1/_2$ cups	**grated Monterey Jack cheese**
2 cups	**grated carrots**
1$^1/_2$ cups	**sliced celery**
4 to 6	**hard-boiled eggs,** sliced

For individual salads, equally divide lettuce onto plates, then layer ingredients in the order listed above. Serve with dressing of choice. Makes 6–8 servings.

BBQ CHICKEN SALAD

2 cups **french-fried onions**
I bag (10 ounces) **romaine lettuce**
I can (15 ounces) **black beans,** rinsed and drained
2 cups **grated sharp cheddar cheese**
I **avocado,** diced
I **pound boneless, skinless chicken breasts,** cooked and cubed
I to 2 cups **barbecue sauce**
ranch dressing

To make onions crispy, microwave 30 seconds, then set aside. Equally divide lettuce onto individual plates, then layer beans, cheese, avocado, and chicken over top. Drizzle barbecue sauce over chicken and then sprinkle onions over top. Serve with ranch dressing on the side. Makes 4–6 servings.

MARINATED BEEF SALAD

$^3/_4$ pound **cooked roast beef,** sliced
2 tablespoons **soy sauce**
1 tablespoon **sesame seeds**
1 tablespoon **lemon juice**
1 clove **garlic,** crushed
1 **small head iceberg or leaf lettuce**
2 **medium tomatoes,** chopped
2 **green onions,** sliced
2 cups **sliced mushrooms**
1 package (14 ounces) **frozen pea pods,** thawed

Dressing:

$^1/_2$ cup **vegetable oil**
$^1/_4$ cup **red wine vinegar**
1 teaspoon **salt**
1 to 2 **garlic cloves,** crushed
pepper

Marinate beef in soy sauce, sesame seeds, lemon juice, and garlic for 4 hours in refrigerator.

In a large bowl, toss everything except dressing ingredients together. Combine dressing ingredients in a separate container and pour over salad just before serving. Toss to coat. Makes 4–6 servings.

JO'S CHICKEN WONTON SALAD

Salad:

3 to 4	**boneless, skinless chicken breasts,** cooked and shredded
1	**head iceberg lettuce,** torn into bite-size pieces
2 cups	**chopped celery**
5 tablespoons	**toasted sesame seeds**
1/4 cup	**toasted sliced almonds**
1 bunch	**cilantro,** chopped
12 to 14	**wonton wrappers,** fried in oil and broken up

Dressing:

6 tablespoons	**rice vinegar**
2 tablespoons	**lemon juice**
1 teaspoon	**white pepper**
1 1/2 teaspoons	**dried mustard**
1/2 cup	**oil**
1 tablespoon	**sesame oil**
4 tablespoons	**sugar**
1 1/2 teaspoons	**salt**

Toss all salad ingredients except wontons together in a large bowl. Combine all dressing ingredients and toss onto salad (but don't saturate) just before serving. Add wontons. Makes 4–6 servings.

ENCHILADA SALAD

I envelope **ranch dressing mix**
$1/2$ cup **mild salsa**
$1/2$ to $3/4$ teaspoon **Tabasco sauce,** or to taste
I **head leafy green lettuce,** torn into
bite-size pieces
$1/2$ to I **red onion,** thinly sliced
I pound **boneless, skinless chicken breasts,**
cubed and cooked
$1/2$ to I cup **enchilada sauce**
I to 2 cups **grated cheddar cheese**
I to 2 cups **crushed Fritos corn chips**

Make ranch dressing according to package directions. Once dressing is set, combine with salsa and Tabasco sauce and chill until ready to serve.

Layer lettuce, onion, and chicken on individual plates. Drizzle enchilada sauce over chicken. Sprinkle cheese and corn chips over top. Serve with salsa ranch dressing on the side. Makes 4–6 servings.

AVOCADO CHICKEN CAESAR SALAD

1	**small avocado**
6 cups	**torn romaine lettuce**
1	**medium tomato,** cut into wedges
2	**chicken breasts,** grilled and sliced
2 to 4 tablespoons	**grated Parmesan cheese**
	Caesar dressing

Peel avocado, remove pit, and then thinly slice. In a large bowl, gently toss all ingredients except dressing. Serve salad with dressing on the side or divide all ingredients except dressing and place onto 4–6 salad plates. Place dressing in a small decorative bowl with a small ladle for serving. Makes 4–6 servings.

VARIATION: Grilled shrimp can be used instead of chicken.

FRUIT 'N' NUT CHICKEN SALAD

1 bag (10 ounces) **mixed salad greens**
1 can (5 ounces) **chicken breast meat,** drained
1 **medium apple,** cored and sliced
1 cup **seedless grapes halves**
$^1/_2$ cup **chopped walnuts or**
slivered almonds
honey mustard or ranch dressing

Divide salad greens between 4–6 plates. Arrange chicken, apple, grapes, and walnuts over top of each salad. Serve with dressing of choice. Makes 4–6 servings.

TORTELLINI SALAD

$^1/_2$ cup **sugar**
$^1/_2$ cup **mayonnaise**
2 teaspoons **cider vinegar**
2 to 3 cups **bite-size broccoli florets**
$^3/_4$ cup **diced roasted red peppers**
1 pound **chicken,** cooked and cubed
1 package (13 ounces) **three-cheese tortellini,** cooked
and cooled
6 to 8 slices **bacon,** cooked and torn into
$^1/_2$-inch pieces
$^1/_2$ cup **sunflower seeds**
$^3/_4$ to 1 cup **crumbled feta cheese**

In a small bowl, combine sugar, mayonnaise, and cider vinegar until smooth and set aside.

In a large bowl, combine broccoli, red peppers, chicken, cooked tortellini, bacon, sunflower seeds, and cheese. Pour dressing over top and gently stir to coat. Chill 1 to 2 hours before serving. Makes 4–6 servings.

VARIATION: To make salad creamier, use $^3/_4$ cup sugar, $^3/_4$ cup mayonnaise, and 1 tablespoon cider vinegar.

MANGO CHICKEN SALAD

1 bag (10 ounces)	**romaine and iceberg mix salad**
2	**chicken breasts,** grilled and sliced
1 cup	**dried cranberries**
1	**mango,** seeded and cubed
$^1/_2$ cup	**slivered almonds**
	poppy seed dressing

Place salad on plates or in bowls, then layer chicken, cranberries, mango, and almonds over top. Serve with poppy seed dressing on the side. Makes 4 servings.

PASTA SALADS

JENNY'S CASHEW BOW-TIE PASTA

12 ounces **bow-tie pasta,** cooked and cooled
$^{1}/_{2}$ to 1 pound **chicken,** cooked and cubed*
1 cup **sliced celery**
1 $^{1}/_{4}$ cups **ranch dressing****
$^{1}/_{2}$ teaspoon **salt**
$^{1}/_{2}$ cup **sauteed mushroom slices**
$^{1}/_{4}$ cup **chopped green onions**
1 cup **frozen peas,** thawed
1 cup **cashews**

Mix pasta, chicken, celery, ranch dressing and salt in a large bowl. Refrigerate 5 hours. Stir in mushrooms, onions, and peas. Sprinkle with cashews and serve. Add more dressing, if necessary. Makes 8–10 servings.

*Saute chicken in light olive oil, salt, and pepper.
**Ranch dressing made from a dry mix tastes best here.

PIZZA PASTA SALAD

12 ounces **penne pasta,** cooked and cooled
30 slices **pepperoni,** halved
1 1/2 to 2 cups **mozzarella cheese,** cubed
1 cup **sliced green olives**
1 **green bell pepper,** diced
1 cup **sliced mushrooms**
1 cup **Italian dressing**
1/4 cup **grated Parmesan cheese**

Combine all ingredients except Parmesan in a bowl. Once combined, sprinkle Parmesan as a garnish over top. Refrigerate 1–2 hours before serving. Add more dressing, if necessary. Makes 8–10 servings.

SHRIMP 'N' SEASHELL SALAD

12 ounces **small shell macaroni,** cooked
and cooled
2 to 3 stalks **celery,** diced
2 cans (4 ounces each) **tiny shrimp,** drained
1 **small onion,** finely chopped
1 to 1½ cups **Miracle Whip**

Mix all ingredients together in a bowl. Refrigerate 1–2 hours. Add more
Miracle Whip before serving, if necessary. Makes 8–10 servings.

PERFECT PICNIC PASTA SALAD

16 ounces **corkscrew pasta,** cooked and cooled
1 1/2 cups **bite-size broccoli florets**
1 **red bell pepper,** diced
1 **green bell pepper,** diced
8 to 12 ounces **cheddar cheese,** cubed
1 can (4 ounces) **sliced black olives**
1/2 **small onion,** finely chopped
1 to 1 1/2 cups **Italian dressing**

Mix all ingredients together in a bowl. Refrigerate 1–2 hours before serving. Add more dressing, if necessary. Makes 8–10 servings.

CHICKEN CAESAR PASTA SALAD

12 to 16 ounces **bow-tie pasta,** cooked and cooled
8 to 10 **boneless, skinless chicken tenders,** cooked and cubed
3 cups **fresh spinach leaves**
1$\frac{1}{2}$ cups **frozen peas,** thawed
1$\frac{1}{2}$ cups **Caesar salad dressing**
salt and pepper, to taste
$\frac{1}{2}$ cup **grated Asiago cheese**

Mix all ingredients except cheese in a bowl. Sprinkle cheese over top. Refrigerate 1–2 hours before serving. Add more dressing, if necessary. Makes 8–10 servings.

TUNA NOODLE PASTA SALAD

12 ounces **corkscrew pasta,** cooked
and cooled
1 can (12 ounces) **white tuna,** drained
1 cup **diced celery**
1 bag (16 ounces) **frozen peas,** thawed
1 **head lettuce,** shredded
1 cup **mayonnaise**
$1/4$ cup **milk**
salt and pepper, to taste

Combine pasta, tuna, celery, peas, and lettuce in a bowl.

In a separate bowl, mix mayonnaise with enough milk to slightly thin it
out. Pour over pasta salad mixture and stir until completely covered.
Season with salt and pepper. Makes 8–10 servings.

CLASSIC MACARONI SALAD

16 ounces **shell macaroni,** cooked and cooled
1 cup **chopped celery**
1/4 cup **finely chopped onion**
1 package (16 ounces) **frozen peas and carrots,** thawed
3 **hard-boiled eggs,** slightly chopped*
3/4 cup **Miracle Whip**
1/2 teaspoon **salt**
1/2 teaspoon **pepper**
paprika

Combine all ingredients except paprika in a bowl. Refrigerate 1–2 hours before serving. Add more Miracle Whip, if needed. Sprinkle paprika over top for colorful garnish. Makes 8–10 servings.

*Slice one egg for decorative garnish on top of salad and then sprinkle with paprika.

SOUTHWEST PASTA SALAD

1 package (12 to 16 ounces) **egg noodles,** cooked
and cooled
1 **red bell pepper,** diced
1 **yellow bell pepper,** diced
1 can (15 ounces) **black beans,** rinsed and drained
1 cup **frozen kernel corn,** thawed
1 cup **grated Monterey Jack or**
pepper jack cheese
1 bottle (12 ounces) **creamy French dressing**

In a bowl, combine all ingredients except dressing. Toss with half the
dressing and chill 1 hour. Gradually add remaining dressing to desired
consistency just before serving. Makes 8–10 servings.

BACON RANCH PASTA SALAD

12 to 16 ounces **curly rotini pasta,** cooked and cooled
2¹/₂ cups **chopped cooked chicken**
¹/₂ cup **real bacon bits**
1¹/₂ cups **ranch dressing**
2¹/₂ cups **fresh bite-size broccoli florets**
1¹/₂ cups **grated medium cheddar cheese**
¹/₃ cup **sunflower seeds**

Mix all ingredients together and chill. Add more dressing, if necessary, before serving. Makes 8–10 servings.

FRUITY BOW-TIE PASTA SALAD

16 ounces **bow-tie pasta,** cooked and cooled
1 cup **craisins**
2 cups **red grapes,** halved
1 can (11 ounces) **mandarin oranges,** drained
1 can (8 ounces) **pineapple tidbits,** drained
³/₄ cup **cashew pieces**
2 **green onions,** chopped
1 cup **diced celery**
1 cup **coleslaw dressing**
¹/₂ cup **mayonnaise**

In a large bowl, combine cooked pasta, craisins, grapes, oranges, pineapple, cashews, onions, and celery.

In a small bowl, combine coleslaw dressing and mayonnaise. Drizzle dressing over salad, and gently toss. Makes 10–12 servings.

ANGIE'S BALSAMIC CHICKEN PASTA SALAD

1 pint **grape tomatoes,** halved
3 tablespoons **chopped cilantro**
1 cup **sliced or coarsely chopped zucchini**
2 to 3 cups **bite-size broccoli florets**
1 can (4 ounces) **sliced black olives**
1/2 cup **chopped onion**
1 bottle (16 ounces) **balsamic vinaigrette dressing,** divided
3 **boneless, skinless chicken breasts,** cut into bite-size pieces
12 ounces **bow-tie pasta,** cooked and cooled
3 cups **fresh spinach**
1 cup **fresh crumbled feta cheese***

Place tomatoes, cilantro, zucchini, broccoli, olives, and onion in a large bowl. Pour about half the balsamic vinaigrette over top and stir. Marinate for 1 hour in the refrigerator.

Preheat oven to 350 degrees. Bake chicken pieces, brushed with a little of the reserved balsamic vinaigrette, for 20–25 minutes, or until done.

Add the chicken, pasta, spinach, and cheese to the vegetable mixture. Use remaining balsamic vinaigrette dressing to moisten pasta to desired consistency. Makes 8–10 servings.

*Asiago or Parmesan cheese may be substituted.

RANCH SHELL PASTA SALAD

1 envelope **ranch salad dressing mix**
1/2 cup **milk**
3/4 cup **mayonnaise**
1 package (16 ounces) **small-shell pasta,** cooked and cooled
1 bag (16 ounces) **frozen peas,** thawed and drained
1/3 cup **sliced green onions**

In a large bowl, combine dressing mix, milk, and mayonnaise. Gently combine pasta, peas, and green onions with ranch mixture. Chill until ready to serve. Makes 10–12 servings.

SUMMER FETA PASTA SALAD

$^1/_2$ **large red bell pepper**
$^1/_2$ **large green bell pepper**
10 to 12 **cherry or grape tomatoes**
1 bag (8 ounces) **rotini or curly pasta,** cooked
and cooled
1 can (10 to 13 ounces) **chicken breast meat,** drained
$^3/_4$ cup **Caesar salad dressing**
$^1/_3$ cup **crumbled feta cheese**

Cut bell peppers into small bite-size pieces. Place tomatoes and peppers into a 2-quart bowl. Add pasta, chicken, and dressing to bowl. Gently stir to combine all ingredients. Sprinkle feta cheese over top. Refrigerate until ready to serve. Makes 4–6 servings.

RED POTATO–PASTA SALAD

6 **red potatoes,** diced and cooked
16 ounces **spiral pasta,** cooked and cooled
1 **yellow bell pepper,** seeded and diced
$^1/_2$ cup **sliced green onions**
$^1/_2$ cup **mayonnaise**
1 cup **ranch dressing**
$^3/_4$ cup **cup real bacon bits**

In a 2-quart saucepan, cover potatoes with water and bring to a boil over high heat. Reduce to medium-low heat and simmer 10–15 minutes or until tender. Drain and rinse potatoes with cold water. Place cooked pasta and potatoes in a large bowl. Stir in bell pepper, green onions, mayonnaise, and ranch dressing. Refrigerate until ready to serve. Stir in bacon bits just before serving. Makes 10–12 servings.

TANGY TRICOLOR PASTA SALAD

1 package (16 ounces) **tricolor spiral pasta,** cooked
and cooled
1/2 cup **chopped red onion**
2 **large tomatoes,** chopped
1 **large cucumber,** peeled and cubed

Dressing:

1 1/4 cups **sugar**
1/2 cup **vinegar**
1 tablespoon **ground mustard**
1 teaspoon **garlic powder**
1/2 teaspoon **salt**

In a large bowl, combine cooked pasta, onion, tomatoes, and cucumber. In a saucepan, heat sugar, vinegar, mustard, garlic powder, and salt together over low heat until sugar dissolves. Pour dressing over pasta mixture and toss to coat. Chill for 2 hours or overnight. Toss again before serving. Makes 10–15 servings.

VARIATION: A green bell pepper, seeded and diced, or chopped cooked ham can be added to this salad.

PRIMAVERA PASTA SALAD

1 box (16 ounces) **bow-tie pasta,** cooked and cooled
4 **Roma tomatoes,** diced*
4 **green onions,** thinly sliced
1 can (4 ounces) **sliced black olives**
1 jar (3 ounces) **green olives,** sliced
1 can (14 ounces) **quartered artichoke hearts,** halved
1 cup **chopped fresh Italian parsley**
2 teaspoons **dried basil**
$^1/_4$ cup **olive oil**
1 bottle (12 ounces) **Italian dressing,** divided
1 cup **pine nuts**
1 to 2 cups **grated Parmesan cheese**
pepper, to taste

In a large bowl, combine pasta, tomatoes, onions, olives, artichoke hearts, parsley, basil, olive oil, and half the Italian dressing, and then chill overnight. Before serving, add remaining dressing to desired consistency. Stir in pine nuts, cheese, and pepper. Makes 8–10 servings.

*You can peel tomatoes first, if desired.

BBQ and Picnic Salads

MOM'S POTATO SALAD

5 to 6 **red potatoes,** cooked and cubed
4 to 5 **hard-boiled eggs,** sliced
$1/2$ cup **diced pickles**
$1/2$ cup **onion,** finely chopped (optional)
1 cup **mayonnaise**
1 cup **sour cream**
1 tablespoon **mustard**
$1/4$ cup **milk**
salt and pepper, to taste

Mix potatoes, eggs, pickles, and onion, if desired, together in a bowl and set aside.

In a separate bowl, combine mayonnaise, sour cream, mustard, and milk until creamy and smooth. Spoon over potato mixture and gently stir until completely covered. Season with salt and pepper. Makes 8–10 servings.

GERMAN POTATO SALAD

6 to 8 **large red potatoes**
1 to 2 **bouillon cubes,** boiled in 1 1/2 cups water
1 tablespoon **Maggi seasoning***
1/8 cup **white vinegar**
1/8 cup **pickle juice**
1/4 **medium onion,** finely chopped (optional)
1/2 cup **vegetable oil**
1 teaspoon **salt**
1 teaspoon **pepper**
3 tablespoons **chopped parsley**
3 slices **pastrami,** chopped
1/2 cup **chopped dill pickles**

Boil potatoes in their skins until fork tender. Peel and allow to cool a little. Slice and add all ingredients except pastrami and dill pickles to potatoes, and then mix well. The salad should be quite moist. Taste and adjust seasoning, if desired. Sprinkle pastrami and pickles over top for garnish. Can be eaten cold or warm. Makes 6–8 servings.

*Available at Albertson's or other large chain grocery stores.

BAKED POTATO SALAD

6 **red or new potatoes,** cooked and cubed
¹/₂ cup **finely chopped onion**
1 cup **mayonnaise**
1 cup **sour cream**
1 tablespoon **mustard**
¹/₄ cup **milk**
salt and pepper, to taste
1 pound **bacon,** cooked and crumbled
2 cups **grated cheddar cheese**
chives, chopped

Mix potatoes and onion together in a bowl and set aside.

In a separate bowl, combine mayonnaise, sour cream, mustard, and milk until creamy and smooth. Spoon over potato mixture and gently stir until completely covered. Season with salt and pepper. Just before serving, layer bacon and cheese over top. Garnish with chives. Makes 8–10 servings.

CHICKEN AND GRAPE SALAD

5 to 6 cups **cooked and cubed chicken**
1 to 1 1/2 cups **seedless red grape halves**
1/2 cup **slivered almonds or cashew halves**
1 to 1 1/2 cups **mayonnaise**
salt and pepper, to taste
large lettuce leaves or croissants

Mix chicken, grapes, celery, and nuts together in a bowl. Stir in mayonnaise gradually to desired consistency. (Use more or less mayonnaise, as desired.) Season with salt and pepper. When ready to serve, scoop individual servings onto large lettuce leaves or in a croissant. Makes 8–10 servings.

EGG SALAD WITH BACON

1/2 cup **chopped celery**
1/3 cup **mayonnaise**
2 to 3 teaspoons **mustard**
1/4 to 1/2 teaspoon **Tabasco sauce**
8 **hard-boiled eggs,** peeled and chopped
salt and pepper, to taste
5 slices **bacon,** cooked and crumbled
8 slices **bread**

In a bowl, combine all ingredients except bacon. Add bacon to mixture just before serving, or sprinkle over top. Evenly divide egg mixture and spoon over 4 slices of bread. Cover with remaining slices. Makes 4 servings.

VARIATION: Add sliced cheese and lettuce to make a more filling sandwich.

HAWAIIAN COLESLAW

³/4 cup **mayonnaise**
2 tablespoons **vinegar**
2 tablespoons **sugar**
1 to 2 tablespoons **milk**
4 cups **shredded cabbage**
³/4 cup **shredded carrots**
1 can (8 ounces) **pineapple tidbits,** drained
paprika (optional)

In a small bowl, combine mayonnaise, vinegar, sugar, and milk, then set aside.

In a separate bowl, combine cabbage, carrots, and pineapple. Pour dressing on top and stir to coat. Sprinkle paprika over top, if desired, and then refrigerate 1–2 hours before serving. Makes 6–8 servings.

ORIENTAL CASHEW COLESLAW

1 package (3 ounces) **oriental ramen noodles,** with
seasoning packet
1 bag (16 ounces) **coleslaw salad**
$^1/_3$ cup **cashew pieces**
$^1/_4$ cup **sliced green onions**
$^1/_2$ cup **olive or Canola oil**
$^1/_3$ cup **apple cider or rice vinegar**
3 tablespoons **sugar**

Crush noodles into small pieces, reserving seasoning packet for dressing.

In a large bowl, toss crushed noodles, coleslaw, cashews, and onions.

In a small bowl, combine oil, vinegar, sugar, and seasoning packet.
Pour dressing over coleslaw mixture. Toss to coat. Serve immediately.
Makes 6–8 servings.

MOM'S TUNA SALAD

I can (6 ounces) **tuna in water,** drained*
3 tablespoons **Miracle Whip**
$^1/_4$ cup **sweet pickle relish**
I stalk **celery,** chopped
2 tablespoons **chopped onion**

Combine all ingredients. Serve over crackers, a bed of lettuce, or a slice of bread. Makes 2–3 servings.

VARIATION: Spread tuna salad over sliced bread, add a slice of cheddar cheese over top, and place in the broiler to melt.

*A can of salmon can be used in place of tuna.

EASY CRAB SALAD

1/2 cup **diced green bell pepper**
1/2 cup **chopped onion**
2 tablespoons **butter**
I can (6 ounces) **crabmeat,** drained
1/2 cup **mayonnaise**
croissants or lettuce
paprika

Saute bell pepper and onion in butter for 3–4 minutes until vegetables soften. Stir in crabmeat and saute an additional 3 minutes. Remove from heat and stir in mayonnaise. Serve hot or cover and chill for 2 hours or overnight before serving. Serve on croissants or over bed of lettuce. Sprinkle with paprika, to garnish. Makes 2 servings.

TURKEY AND APPLE SALAD

I can (5 ounces) **turkey,** drained*
$^1/_2$ cup **diced apple**
$^1/_4$ cup **diced celery**
$^1/_4$ cup **Miracle Whip** or **mayonnaise**

Stir all ingredients together. Cover and chill for 1–3 hours before serving.
Serve on croissants or over bed of lettuce. Makes 2–3 servings.

* Leftover cooked turkey can also be used in this recipe.

Veggie Salads

TOMATO AND MOZZARELLA SALAD

3 to 4 **large tomatoes,** cut in $^1/_4$-inch slices
2 pounds **fresh mozzarella cheese,** cut in
$^1/_4$-inch slices
$^1/_4$ cup **freshly chopped basil**
balsamic vinaigrette
salt and pepper

Alternate tomato and mozzarella slices on a serving tray. Sprinkle with basil. Drizzle desired amount of balsamic vinaigrette over top. Sprinkle with salt and pepper. Makes 6–8 servings.

CHILLED CUCUMBER SALAD

3 **cucumbers,** peeled and sliced
$^1/_4$ cup **chopped onion**
2 teaspoons **dill**
1 teaspoon **salt**
1 teaspoon **sugar**
$^1/_2$ cup **balsamic vinaigrette**

Place all ingredients in a bowl. Toss well. Chill 1 hour or overnight.
Makes 5–6 servings.

VARIATION: Cucumbers can be cut in half, seeded, and cut into bite-size
pieces for this recipe.

FRUITY BROCCOLI SALAD

Dressing:

1 cup **mayonnaise**
2 tablespoons **red wine vinegar**
$^1/_2$ cup **sugar**

Salad:

5 cups **broccoli florets,** cut into
bite-size pieces
1 cup **red grape halves**
1 cup **sliced or quartered strawberries**
$^1/_2$ to 1 **red onion,** chopped or thinly sliced
1 pound **bacon,** cooked and crumbled
$2^1/_2$ cups **grated sharp cheddar cheese**
$^1/_2$ cup **sunflower seeds**

In a bowl, combine all dressing ingredients and set aside.

In a large bowl, combine all salad ingredients. Pour dressing over top
and stir. Refrigerate 1 hour before serving. Makes 8–10 servings.

CHUNKY VEGGIE SALAD

$^1/_2$ pound **baby carrots,** halved
1 **medium cucumber,** peeled, halved, and sliced
1 pint **grape tomatoes**
1 cup **sliced celery**
1 small bunch **radishes,** sliced or quartered
2 cups **sugar snap peas**
1 to 2 cups **broccoli or cauliflower florets,** cut into bite-size pieces
ranch dressing

Mix all ingredients together in a bowl. Serve with ranch dressing or a dressing of choice on the side. Makes 10–12 servings.

FOUR-BEAN SALAD

Dressing:

¹/₂ cup	**vinegar**
¹/₂ cup	**red wine vinegar**
¹/₂ cup	**light olive oil**
I cup	**sugar**

Salad:

2 cans (15 ounces each)	**wax beans,** drained
I can (15 ounces)	**garbanzo beans,** drained
2 cans (15 ounces each)	**whole green beans,** drained
2 cans (15 ounces each)	**red kidney beans,** rinsed and drained
I	**small red onion,** thinly sliced
I	**green bell pepper,** thinly sliced

In a bowl, combine all dressing ingredients and set aside.

In a separate bowl, combine all salad ingredients. Pour dressing over top and stir. Refrigerate 24 hours, stirring occasionally. When ready to serve, drain dressing or serve with a slotted spoon. Makes 10–12 servings.

CAULIFLOWER-SHRIMP SALAD

1 **small head cauliflower**
$^1/_2$ cup **mayonnaise**
1 teaspoon **mustard**
1 tablespoon **ketchup**
1 tablespoon **chopped fresh parsley**
1 tablespoon **chopped chives**
$^1/_4$ teaspoon **salt**
pepper, to taste
$^1/_2$ pound **small cooked shrimp** (or 1 can shrimp)

Divide cauliflower into bite-size pieces and cook until tender in salted water.

In a bowl, combine mayonnaise, mustard, ketchup, parsley, chives, salt, and pepper. Combine cauliflower, shrimp, and dressing mixture. Toss and refrigerate at least 30 minutes before serving. Makes 4 servings.

CRUNCHY PEA SALAD

2 cups **frozen peas,** thawed
$^3/_4$ cup **sliced or diced celery**
2 cups **bite-size cauliflower florets**
$^1/_4$ cup **sliced green onions**
$^1/_2$ cup **sliced fresh mushrooms**
1 cup **cashews**
$1^1/_2$ cups **grated cheddar cheese**
8 to 10 slices **bacon,** cooked and crumbled
$^1/_2$ to 1 cup **ranch dressing**

In a bowl, combine all ingredients. Add more dressing, if needed. Sprinkle additional green onions and bacon over top as garnish, if desired. Makes 8–10 servings.

BACON BROCCOLI SALAD

6 cups **fresh broccoli,** coarsely chopped
²/₃ cup **real bacon bits***
2 cups **shredded sharp cheddar cheese**
¹/₂ **large red onion,** chopped
¹/₄ cup **apple cider vinegar**
2 tablespoons **sugar**
1 teaspoon **black pepper**
1 teaspoon **salt**
²/₃ cup **mayonnaise**
1 teaspoon **lemon juice**

In a large bowl, toss broccoli, bacon, cheese, and onion together.

In a separate bowl, combine vinegar, sugar, pepper, salt, mayonnaise, and lemon juice. Mix dressing into salad. Cover and refrigerate until ready to serve. Makes 6–8 servings.

VARIATIONS: Add ²/₃ cup raisins, craisins, or sunflower seeds to salad.

*Substitute 10–12 slices of bacon, cooked and crumbled, in place of real bacon bits, if desired.

CAULIFLOWER—GREEN PEA SALAD

1 **head cauliflower**
1 bag (16 ounces) **frozen peas,** thawed
1 cup **sour cream**
1/3 cup **mayonnaise**
1 envelope **ranch dressing mix**

Clean and cut cauliflower into bite-size pieces. Combine cauliflower and peas in a large bowl.

In a small bowl, combine sour cream, mayonnaise, and ranch dressing mix. Toss cauliflower and peas together with ranch mixture. Chill until ready to serve. Makes 8–10 servings.

MEXICORN BEAN SALAD

3 tablespoons **olive oil**
3 tablespoons **vinegar**
I tablespoon **dry ranch dressing mix**
I can (16 ounces) **kidney beans,** rinsed and drained
I can (15 ounces) **black beans,** rinsed and drained
I can (11 ounces) **Mexicorn,** drained
$^1/_4$ cup **sliced green onions**

In a salad bowl, mix oil, vinegar, and ranch dressing mix together until powder is thoroughly dissolved. Fold beans, corn, and onions into dressing until evenly coated. Cover and refrigerate until serving. Makes 6–8 servings.

ENSALADA CHILENA

1 **medium red onion,** julienned
5 **medium tomatoes,** sliced
oil, to taste
2 tablespoons **chopped cilantro**
salt, to taste

Place cut onion in a bowl and cover with water 2–3 hours to soften. Drain onion. Stir tomato slices and onion together. Lightly drizzle olive or vegetable oil over mixture. Sprinkle with cilantro and salt. Stir again. Serve immediately or chill until ready to serve. Makes 8–10 servings.

*Onions can soak all day.

BELL PEPPER SALAD

1 **red bell pepper,** diced
1 **yellow or orange bell pepper,** diced
1 **green bell pepper,** diced
1/2 cup **chopped red onion**
1/4 cup **chopped fresh parsley**
1/2 cup **balsamic vinaigrette**

Combine all ingredients in a serving bowl. Cover and chill until ready to serve. Makes 6–8 servings.

RANCH CAULIFLOWER AND BROCCOLI SALAD

1 **medium head cauliflower**
¹/₂ **medium head broccoli**
¹/₃ cup **sliced green onions**
1 **red or yellow bell pepper,** diced
¹/₂ cup **raisins**
1 envelope **ranch dressing mix**
1 cup **mayonnaise**
1 cup **plain yogurt**

Clean and cut vegetables into bite-size pieces. Place vegetables and raisins in a large bowl. Combine ranch seasoning, mayonnaise, and yogurt. Stir ranch mixture into vegetables until evenly covered. Refrigerate until ready to serve. Makes 6–8 servings.

FRUIT SALADS

SWEET-AND-SOUR FRUIT SALAD

Glaze:

6 tablespoons **frozen orange juice concentrate,** thawed
$^1/_2$ cup **water**
$^1/_8$ teaspoon **vanilla extract**

Salad:

1 **large green apple**
1 **large banana**
2 **oranges**
3 **kiwifruits**
1 cup **sliced strawberries**
1 cup **seedless red grapes**

In a bowl, combine glaze ingredients and set aside. Cut apple and banana into bite-size pieces and add to glaze. Toss to coat to prevent browning. Peel and cut oranges and place in a large bowl. Peel and slice kiwifruits, then cut slices in half. Add all remaining fruit to glaze and stir to coat. Makes 6–8 servings.

MELISSA'S CREAMY FRUIT SALAD

1 **large peach**
4 **kiwifruits**
1 **large banana**
2 **large Fuji or Gala apples**
1 1/2 cups **sliced strawberries**
1 cup **seedless red or green grapes halves**
1 container (6 ounces) **Yoplait blackberry yogurt**
1 to 1 1/2 cups **whipped topping**
Raspberries or blackberries

Peel and cut the peach, then place in a bowl. Peel and slice kiwifruits and banana and add to bowl. Cut apples into bite-size pieces and add to bowl. Gently stir in strawberries and grapes.

In a separate bowl, fold yogurt and whipped topping together, then gently stir into fruit. Garnish with fresh raspberries or blackberries on top. Add more whipped topping, if needed. Makes 6–8 servings.

COOL PEAR SALAD

I can (29 ounces) **pears,** juice reserved
I small box **lime or lemon gelatin**
I cup **hot pear juice** (use juice from can)
I package (8 ounces) **cream cheese,** room temperature
4 tablespoons **milk**
2 cups **whipped topping**

In a bowl, mash pears with fork. In a separate bowl, dissolve gelatin in hot pear juice and let sit until soupy. Make up the difference with water if there isn't enough pear juice in the can.

In another bowl, mash cream cheese and milk with a fork or spoon until smooth. Combine pears, gelatin mixture, and cream cheese mixture. Fold in I cup whipped topping. Spoon into a serving bowl and smooth top. Chill at least 2 hours, or until firm. Spread remaining whipped topping over top and serve. Makes 8–10 servings.

BERRIES 'N' CRÈME SALAD

Crème:

1 cup	**heavy whipping cream**
1/2 cup	**sugar**
1 teaspoon	**unflavored gelatin**
1 tablespoon	**cold water**
1/8 cup	**boiling water**
1 cup	**light sour cream**
1 teaspoon	**vanilla**

Salad:

2 cups	**frozen blackberries**
2 cups	**frozen raspberries**
1 to 2 cups	**strawberry halves**
1 cup	**blueberries**

In a small saucepan, heat cream and sugar together until sugar is dissolved. In a separate bowl, combine gelatin with cold water, then boiling water. Combine cream mixture and gelatin mixture in a bowl. With a spoon, whip in sour cream and vanilla. Refrigerate 24 hours or overnight.

Gently layer berries into a 9 x 13-inch glass casserole dish. Cover and refrigerate 24 hours or overnight. When frozen berries thaw, the juices blend together and make a tart sauce. When ready to serve, remove berries and crème from refrigerator. Gently mix fruit to ensure it is completely covered in sauce. Drizzle crème over top, as desired, or serve individual portions by first spooning berries into parfait glasses, then drizzling with crème. Makes 6–8 servings.

PUCKERED-UP CITRUS SALAD

2 **oranges**
2 **small grapefruit**
2 cups **pineapple chunks**
1 **pomegranate,** seeded*
1 **lime,** thinly sliced

Peel and cut oranges and grapefruit into bite-size pieces and put in a bowl. Stir in pineapple chunks and pomegranate seeds. Garnish with lime slices. Makes 4–6 servings.

*2 cups red grapes may be substituted, or added in addition to pomegranate seeds.

MELON DELIGHT SALAD

1 **seedless watermelon,** cut in half*
2 **cantaloupe,** cut in half and seeded
1 **honeydew melon,** cut in half and seeded
2 to 3 cups **seedless red grapes**

With a melon baller, scoop out balls from each melon and drop into a large bowl. Stir in grapes and serve. Makes 10–12 servings.

*Once flesh is scooped out of watermelon, the rind shell may be used as the serving bowl.

STRAWBERRY– SOUR CREAM SALAD

I large box	**strawberry gelatin**
I cup	**boiling water**
I box	**frozen strawberries,** partially thawed
I can (8 ounces)	**crushed pineapple,** drained
2	**bananas,** mashed
	walnuts
I to I¹/₂ cups	**sour cream**

Mix gelatin and boiling water in a bowl, then add strawberries. Next add pineapple, bananas, and walnuts. Pour half the mixture into a bowl and spread sour cream over top. Pour remaining gelatin mixture over top. Chill until set. Makes 8 servings.

CHERRY WALDORF SALAD

1 **large Granny Smith apple**
1 **large Fuji apple**
$^1/_2$ cup **cherry-flavored dried
cranberries**
$^1/_2$ cup **chopped pecans,** divided
2 containers (6 ounces each) **cherry yogurt**

Cut apples into bite-size pieces and mix in a bowl with dried cranberries and half the pecans. Stir in yogurt and sprinkle remaining nuts over top. Makes 4–6 servings.

DAD'S FAVORITE FRUIT SALAD

1 small box **strawberry gelatin**
1 large **banana,** sliced
1 1/2 cups **sliced strawberries**
1 cup **blueberries**
2 to 3 cups **mini marshmallows**
1 small container (8 ounces) **whipped topping**

Make gelatin in a large bowl according to package directions. Once set, layer banana, strawberries, blueberries, and marshmallows over top and then stir together. Gently fold in whipped topping until well coated. Makes 6–8 servings.

HONEY-LIME FRUIT SALAD

4 cups **pineapple chunks**
1 can (15 ounces) **mandarin oranges,** drained
2 large **bananas,** sliced
1 pound **sliced strawberries**
6 **kiwifruits,** peeled and sliced
1/4 cup **lime juice**
1 tablespoon **honey**
1/4 cup **pineapple juice**
1 to 2 tablespoons **lime zest**

In a large bowl, toss all fruit together.

In a separate bowl, combine lime juice, honey, pineapple juice, and lime zest. Pour over fruit and stir to coat. Chill before serving. Makes 6 servings.

LAYERED FRUIT SALAD

I container (6 ounces) **strawberry yogurt**
4 ounces **cream cheese,** softened
2 tablespoons **sugar**
I teaspoon **lemon juice**
2 cups **cantaloupe chunks**
2 cups **sliced strawberries**
2 cups **sliced kiwifruits**
I pint **fresh raspberries**

In a small bowl, mix yogurt, cream cheese, sugar, and lemon juice with a hand-mixer until smooth, then set aside.

In a small glass trifle bowl, spread cantaloupe over bottom. Arrange strawberries over top, followed by kiwifruits, and finishing with raspberries. Evenly spread yogurt mixture over top and serve. Makes 4–6 servings.

GRAPE NUTS SALAD

1 package (8 ounces) **cream cheese,** softened
1 cup **sour cream**
$^1/_2$ cup **sugar**
1 teaspoon **vanilla**
2 pounds **green seedless grapes**
2 pounds **red seedless grapes**
1 cup **Grape Nuts cereal**
brown sugar

In a large bowl, combine cream cheese, sour cream, sugar, and vanilla with a hand mixer. Stir in grapes until completely coated. Sprinkle Grape Nuts over top to cover, then sprinkle brown sugar evenly over Grape Nuts. Makes 10–12 servings.

MANGO FRUIT SALAD

1 pound **strawberries**
1 pound **grapes,** halved
3 **kiwifruits,** peeled and sliced
1 **mango,** peeled, seeded, and sliced

Wash strawberries and grapes. Remove stems and cut each strawberry in half. Combine all fruit in a large bowl. Serve immediately. Store any leftovers in the refrigerator. Makes 4–6 servings.

ALMOND CRAN-APPLE SALAD

3 **green apples**
cored and diced*
1/3 cup **dried cranberries**
1/4 cup **dried cherries,** chopped
I container (8 ounces) **vanilla yogurt**
1/4 cup **sliced almonds**

In a serving bowl, mix together apples, cranberries, cherries, and yogurt. Sprinkle almond slices over the salad. Serve immediately or store in refrigerator. Makes 3–4 servings.

*To prevent apples from changing color, dip in lemon juice.

STRAWBERRY-BANANA SALAD

I pound **fresh strawberries**
¹/₂ pound **seedless green or red grapes**
2 to 3 **bananas,** peeled and sliced
I container (8 ounces) **strawberry yogurt***
whipped topping

Wash strawberries and grapes. Remove stems and cut each strawberry in half. Cut grapes in half. Place strawberries and grapes in a serving bowl. Add sliced bananas. Stir in yogurt. Serve immediately. Garnish individual servings with a dollop of whipped topping. Makes 4–6 servings.

* Lemon, vanilla, or strawberry-banana flavored yogurt can also be used.

FANCIFUL FRUIT SALAD

I can (20 ounces) **pineapple chunks,** with liquid
I small box **instant cheesecake pudding**
I can (29 ounces) **fruit cocktail,** drained
I can (11 ounces) **mandarin oranges,** drained
I **banana,** sliced
I **apple,** diced
whipped topping (optional)

In a punch bowl, mix together juice from pineapple and instant pudding. Fold fruit into pudding mixture. Top with whipped topping, if desired. Makes 6–8 servings.

VARIATION: Try vanilla, banana, or lemon instant pudding in place of cheesecake-flavored pudding.

POPPY SEED–
CANTALOUPE SALAD

1 **medium cantaloupe,** cut into
bite-size pieces
1 to 1 1/2 cups **seedless grapes,** halved
1/2 cup **poppy seed dressing**
1/4 cup **sliced green onions**
1/2 cup **real bacon bits**

In a large bowl, toss cantaloupe and grapes together. Refrigerate until
ready to serve. Before serving, toss salad with poppy seed dressing.
Sprinkle green onions and bacon over top. Makes 6–8 servings.

DESSERT SALADS

PISTACHIO SALAD

1 small box **instant pistachio pudding mix**
1 can (8 ounces) **crushed pineapple,** with juice
1 container (8 ounces) **whipped topping,** thawed
2 to 3 cups **mini marshmallows**
1 cup **cottage cheese**
chopped pistachios

Combine pudding mix and pineapple with juice together in a bowl. Stir in whipped topping, marshmallows, and cottage cheese. Garnish with pistachios. Refrigerate 1–2 hours before serving. Makes 6–8 servings.

FLUFFY LIME SALAD

1 large box **lime gelatin**
1 cup **boiling water**
1 can (5 ounces) **evaporated milk,** very cold*
2 cups **crushed graham crackers**

Dissolve lime gelatin in boiling water in a bowl, then refrigerate 20–25 minutes, or until it starts to set. Pour milk into a chilled bowl and whip with chilled beaters until mixture forms stiff peaks, about 5 minutes. Gently stir in gelatin mixture until well blended. Sprinkle half the crushed graham crackers into bottom of an 8 x 8-inch pan, then carefully spoon lime fluff over top and spread evenly, being careful not to pull up graham cracker crumbs. Sprinkle remaining graham cracker crumbs over top and refrigerate 1–2 hours before serving. Makes 6 servings.

*Chill by placing can in freezer 20–30 minutes. You should also place bowl and beaters in the freezer to chill.

DREAMY GELATIN SALAD

1 large box **gelatin,** any flavor
2 cups **boiling water**
1 cup **cold water**
8 ounces **cream cheese,** softened
1 cup **vanilla ice cream,** softened
1 container (8 ounces) **frozen whipped topping,**
thawed and divided
crushed graham crackers, optional

Mix gelatin and boiling water together in a bowl until dissolved. Add cold water, cream cheese, ice cream, and half the whipped topping. Mix with a hand mixer until creamy and smooth. Pour mixture into a 9 x 13-inch pan and refrigerate 2–3 hours. Top with remaining whipped topping. Sprinkle crushed graham crackers over top as a garnish, if desired. Makes 8–10 servings.

BANANA CREAM SALAD

2 small boxes **banana cream pudding**
3 1/2 cups **milk**
30 **vanilla wafers,** divided
2 **bananas,** sliced
1 container (8 ounces) **frozen whipped topping,**
thawed

Prepare pudding mixes with milk by following the pie preparation directions on package. Pour half the pudding into a 9 x 13-inch pan. Break 20 wafers into bite-size pieces evenly over pudding. Pour remaining pudding over top. Chill until set. When ready to serve, slice bananas and layer over pudding. Spread whipped topping over bananas, then break remaining wafers over top. Makes 10–12 servings.

JESSICA'S CITRUS CREAM SALAD

1 large box **cook & serve lemon pudding**
1 large box **orange gelatin**
1 container (8 ounces) **whipped topping**

Make pudding according to package directions and set aside, keeping warm.

In a bowl, make gelatin according to package directions. While gelatin is still warm, pour into warm pudding and mix well. Pour in a 9 x 13-inch pan and chill 3–4 hours, or until set. Spread a thick layer of whipped topping over top. Makes 8–10 servings.

BEST EVER FROG-EYE SALAD

1 cup	**sugar**
1/2 teaspoon	**salt**
2 tablespoons	**flour**
3	**egg yolks**
1 1/2 cups	**pineapple juice** (drained from can)*
1 1/2 cups	**ancini di pepe pasta**
1 to 2 cans (20 ounces each)	**pineapple tidbits,** drained with juice reserved
2 cans (6 ounces)	**mandarin oranges,** drained
1 bag (16 ounces)	**mini marshmallows**
1 container (12 ounces)	**frozen whipped topping,** thawed

Combine sugar, salt, flour, egg yolks, and pineapple juice over medium heat until slightly thick. Boil pasta according to package directions, then drain, rinse, and cool. Add to cooked mixture and stir. Chill 6 hours. Add pineapple, mandarin oranges, marshmallows, and whipped topping. Refrigerate 1–2 hours before serving. Makes 10–12 servings.

*If pineapple juice drained from pineapple tidbits doesn't measure 1 1/2 cups, combine with juice drained from mandarin oranges.

ROCKY ROAD SALAD

1 large box **instant chocolate pudding**
4 ounces **whipped topping**
2$\frac{1}{2}$ cups **mini marshmallows**
$\frac{3}{4}$ cup **chopped walnuts**
$\frac{1}{2}$ cup **mini chocolate chips**

Make pudding according to package directions and chill until set. Fold in whipped topping, then stir in remaining ingredients. Makes 6–8 servings.

SNICKERS SALAD

5 **Snickers bars,** cut into bite-size pieces
4 **Fuji apples,** cut into bite-size pieces
I container (8 ounces) **frozen whipped topping,** thawed
caramel ice cream topping

Mix all ingredients together except caramel and chill. Lightly drizzle caramel over top just before serving. Makes 6–8 servings.

REFRESHING ICE CREAM SALAD

1 bag (12 ounces) **frozen raspberries**
$^1/_2$ gallon **pineapple sherbet,** slightly softened
2 to 3 **bananas**

Mash raspberries into softened sherbet, then slice bananas and gently stir in. Serve in parfait glasses. Garnish with a few fresh raspberries, if desired. Makes 10–12 servings.

CHERRY-PINEAPPLE SALAD

I can (21 ounces) **cherry pie filling**
I can (20 ounces) **crushed pineapple,** drained
I can (14 ounces) **sweetened condensed milk**
1 1/2 cups **mini marshmallows**
8 ounces **frozen whipped topping,** thawed

In a large bowl, combine pie filling, pineapple, condensed milk, and marshmallows. Gently fold whipped topping into salad. Garnish with fresh cherries or chopped pecans, if desired. Chill until ready to serve. Makes 10–12 servings.

TROPICAL AMBROSIA SALAD

I can (15 ounces) **mandarin oranges,** drained
I can (8 ounces) **crushed pineapple,** drained
1 1/4 cups **coconut**
2 cups **mini marshmallows**
I container (8 ounces) **whipped topping**

In a large serving bowl, combine oranges, pineapple, coconut, and marshmallows. Gently stir whipped topping into salad. Chill for at least I hour before serving. Garnish with chopped pecans or maraschino cherries, if desired. This recipe can be made the night before serving. Makes 6–8 servings.

PEACHY GELATIN SALAD

I large box **peach gelatin**
2 cups **boiling water**
1 1/2 cups **cold water**
I can (15 ounces) **sliced peaches,** drained
1 1/2 cups **mini marshmallows**
8 ounces **whipped topping**

Stir gelatin mix into boiling water until dissolved. Stir in cold water.
Refrigerate 2 hours or overnight. Chop gelatin into small pieces and
place in a large bowl. Dice peaches into bite-size pieces. Stir peaches,
marshmallows, and whipped topping into gelatin. Chill until ready to
serve. Makes 8–10 servings.

GRANDMA'S STRAWBERRY PRETZEL SALAD

2 cups **chopped pretzels**
²/₃ cup **butter** or **margarine,** melted
4 tablespoons **sugar**
8 ounces **cream cheese,** softened
I cup **sugar**
8 ounces **whipped topping**
2 boxes (3 ounces each) **strawberry gelatin**
1¹/₂ cups **boiling water**
2 cartons (10 ounces each) **frozen strawberries in syrup,** thawed

Preheat oven to 400 degrees.

Mix pretzels, butter, and sugar together. Press into bottom of a 9 x 13-inch glass pan. Bake 6 minutes and then cool.

In a bowl, mix cream cheese, sugar, and whipped topping. Spread over pretzel crust. Combine strawberry gelatin and boiling water until gelatin dissolves. Stir in strawberries and spread mixture over cream layer. Chill 3–4 hours until set. Makes 10–12 servings.

VARIATION: Raspberries and raspberry gelatin may be used instead of strawberries and strawberry gelatin.

GRANDMA DIRCKS' ORANGE CREAM SALAD

1 small box **orange gelatin**
1 small box **cook & serve vanilla pudding**
1 small box **tapioca pudding**
3 cups **cold water**
1 can (11 ounces) **mandarin oranges,** drained
12 ounces **whipped topping**

In a soup pan, combine gelatin, puddings, and water. Bring to a boil, stirring consistently. Boil 2 minutes. Remove from heat and cool to room temperature. Stir in oranges. Transfer salad to a glass bowl. Gently fold in whipped topping, reserving dollop to garnish top. Refrigerate until ready to serve. Makes 8–10 servings.

TROPICAL COOKIE SALAD

2 small boxes	**instant vanilla pudding mix**
2 cups	**buttermilk**
12 ounces	**frozen whipped topping,** thawed
1 can (20 ounces)	**crushed pineapple,** drained
2	**bananas,** sliced
2 cans (11 ounces each)	**mandarin oranges,** drained
1/2 package (11.5 ounces)	**fudge-striped cookies**

In a large bowl, combine pudding and buttermilk. Gently fold whipped topping into pudding mixture. Stir in pineapple, bananas, and oranges. Chill until ready to serve. Just before serving, break cookies into bite-size pieces and sprinkle over salad. Makes 8–10 servings.

VARIATIONS: In place of fudge-striped cookies, sprinkle crushed chocolate sandwich cookies or Twix candy bars, cut into bite-size pieces, over salad before serving.

PINEAPPLE PRETZEL SALAD

2 cups **crushed pretzels**
²/₃ cup **butter or margarine,** melted
1 cup **sugar,** divided
1 can (20 ounces) **crushed pineapple,** with juice
2 tablespoons **cornstarch**
1 package (8 ounces) **cream cheese,** softened
8 ounces **frozen whipped topping,** thawed

Preheat oven to 400 degrees.

Combine crushed pretzels, butter, and ¹/₂ cup sugar. Press into bottom of a 9 x 13-inch glass pan. Bake for 6 minutes. Allow crust to cool.

In a small saucepan, combine pineapple with juice, remaining sugar, and cornstarch. Bring to a boil, stirring constantly. Allow pineapple mixture to cool. Spread cooled pineapple mixture over pretzel crust. Mix cream cheese and whipped topping and spread over pineapple mixture. Chill for 2 hours or overnight. Garnish with chopped nuts, if desired. Makes 10–12 servings.

BONUS SECTION: DRESSINGS

FAMILY FAVORITE DRESSING

$^1/_2$ cup **light olive oil**
$^1/_4$ cup **sugar**
3 tablespoons **cider vinegar**
1 tablespoon **minced fresh parsley**
$^1/_2$ teaspoon **salt**
$^1/_4$ teaspoon **pepper**

Combine all ingredients together in a bowl. Serve over your favorite green salad. Store dressing in refrigerator.

LIME VINAIGRETTE DRESSING

$^1/_4$ cup **light olive oil**
$^1/_4$ cup **lime juice**
2 teaspoons **sugar**
$^1/_2$ teaspoon **grated lime peel**
$^1/_4$ teaspoon **salt**

Combine all ingredients together in a bowl. Serve over your favorite green salad. Store dressing in refrigerator.

HONEY MUSTARD DRESSING

1 container (6 ounces) **plain yogurt**
$^1/_3$ cup **light mayonnaise**
$^1/_3$ cup **honey**
$^1/_4$ cup **Dijon mustard**
2 tablespoons **mustard**
$4^1/_2$ teaspoons **cider vinegar**

Combine all ingredients together in a bowl. Refrigerate 1–2 hours before serving. Serve over your favorite green salad. Store dressing in refrigerator.

CREAMY ITALIAN DRESSING

$^1/_4$ teaspoon **oregano**
$^1/_4$ teaspoon **garlic**
$^1/_4$ teaspoon **onion powder**
1 cup **low-fat cottage cheese**
$^1/_3$ cup **buttermilk**
1 teaspoon **lemon juice**

Combine all ingredients together in a blender. Serve over your favorite green salad. Store dressing in refrigerator.

QUICK FRENCH DRESSING

1 can (10.75 ounces) **condensed tomato soup**
1 cup **sugar**
1 cup **vegetable or olive oil**
1 cup **vinegar**

Combine all ingredients in the blender. Chill until ready to serve over your favorite green salad.

CREAMY RASPBERRY DRESSING

8 ounces **plain yogurt**
$^3/_4$ cup **raspberries**
1 tablespoon **balsamic vinegar**
2 teaspoons **sugar**

In a blender, combine all ingredients. Serve over a salad of spinach leaves, thinly sliced red onion, and sliced grilled chicken. Store dressing in refrigerator.

CREAMY PARMESAN DRESSING

$1/4$ cup **milk**
1 cup **light mayonnaise**
2 tablespoons **vinegar**
3 tablespoons **grated Parmesan cheese**

Combine all ingredients together in a bowl. Refrigerate 1–2 hours before serving. Serve on Caesar or any other green salad. Store leftover dressing in refrigerator.

CLASSIC VINAIGRETTE DRESSING

$1/3$ cup **red wine vinegar**
$1/8$ teaspoon **pepper**
3 to 4 teaspoons **sugar**
1 cup **light olive oil**

Combine all ingredients together in a bowl. Serve over your favorite green salad. Store dressing in refrigerator.

MOM'S WESTERN DRESSING

1 cup **ketchup**
1 cup **vegetable or olive oil**
$3/4$ cup **vinegar**
$1 1/4$ cups **sugar**
$1/2$ teaspoon **ground mustard**
$1/2$ teaspoon **paprika**
1 teaspoon **salt**
$1/4$ teaspoon **garlic powder**
$1/2$ teaspoon **barbeque seasoning**

Mix all ingredients together in a blender. Refrigerate 1–2 hours before serving. Serve over green salad or with french fries. Store dressing in refrigerator.

Yum! Each 128 pages, $9.95

Available at bookstores
or directly from GIBBS SMITH, PUBLISHER

1.800.748.5439

www.gibbs-smith.com

ABOUT THE AUTHORS

Melissa Barlow holds a bachelor's degree in journalism from Weber State University. She has been a writer and full-time editor for several years. Melissa enjoys cooking, reading, writing, running, vacationing, watching movies, and relaxing with family and friends. She lives in Bountiful, Utah, with her husband, Todd.

Stephanie Ashcraft, author of the original *101 Things to Do with a Cake Mix*, was raised near Kirklin, Indiana. She received a bachelor's degree in family science and a teaching certificate from Brigham Young University. Since 1998, she has taught cooking classes based on the tips and meals in her cookbooks. She lives in Tucson, Arizona.